THE GHOSTLY TALES OF AMHERST, NEW HAMPSHIRE

Published by Arcadia Children's Books
A Division of Arcadia Publishing, Inc.
Charleston, SC
www.arcadiapublishing.com

Copyright © 2024 by Arcadia Children's Books
All rights reserved

Spooky America is a trademark of Arcadia Publishing, Inc.

First published 2024
Manufactured in the United States

Designed by Jessica Nevins
Images used courtesy of pp. 2, 10, 26, 88, Susanna Hargreaves; all others Shutterstock.com.

ISBN 9781467197861
Library of Congress Control Number: 2024939713

Notice: The information in this book is true and complete to the best of our knowledge. It is offered without guarantee on the part of the author or Arcadia Publishing. The author and Arcadia Publishing disclaim all liability in connection with the use of this book.

All rights reserved. No part of this book may be reproduced or transmitted in any form whatsoever without prior written permission from the publisher except in the case of brief quotations embodied in critical articles and reviews.

Spooky America
The Ghostly Tales of Amherst, New Hampshire

Susanna Hargreaves

VT NEW HAMPSHIRE
ME

NY MA

ATLANTIC OCEAN

AMHERST

Table of Contents & Map Key

Foreword 3

Welcome to Spooky Amherst, New Hampshire! 5

Part 1. Tales Passed Down Through the Years 11

Chapter 1. The Wolves in the Night 12

A Chapter 2. The Young Lovers' Walk 15

Chapter 3. The Spirit Chair 17

Chapter 4. Old Superstitions 19

A Chapter 5. The Mysterious Whipping Block on the Amherst Town Green 23

Part 2. Ghostly Tales 27

B Chapter 6. The Friendly Ghost Who Saved the Barnabas David House 28

A Chapter 7. The Haunting of Town Hall 32

Chapter 8. The Ghosts in the Green House 35

C Chapter 9. Ghosts in the Doctor's Mansion 40

D Chapter 10. The Haunted History of the Aaron Lawrence House 46

Chapter 11. The Ghost of the Spinster 50

E Chapter 12. The Ghosts of the John Watson Tavern 53

Chapter 13. The Ghost in Martin's House 56

Chapter 14. The Reasons Why Karen & Joe Called Ghost Hunters 58

F Chapter 15. The Nightly Rattlings of Mr. Pesterfield 62

G Chapter 16. The Mischievous Ghost at the Blunt House 66

H Chapter 17. The Ghost of Converse Farm 69

I Chapter 18. Children of the Lake 72

Part 3. Indigenous Folklore 77

I Chapter 19. The Lake Spirits 78

J Chapter 20. The River Spirits 81

Chapter 21. The Swamp Woman 84

K Chapter 22. The Spirit of Joe English 86

Part 4. Graves of the Past 89

L Chapter 23. Pauper's Cemetery 90

A Chapter 24. The Old Burying Ground 92

A Chapter 25. Skeletons in the Basement 94

A Ghostly Goodbye 97

You Still Haunt Me, a poem by Susanna Hargreaves 100

Acknowledgments 103

About the Author 105

Bibliography 106

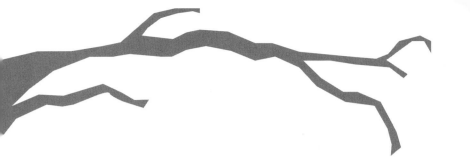

Foreword

DIGGING NEW HAMPSHIRE FROM BENEATH THE SNOW

I semi-joke that my state of New Hampshire is the least-referenced state in the union. It might not be. Idaho could have a right to the crown. Or Delaware. Still, our triangular state is a snowy blank slate to most of the rest of the country.

And that's too bad. Because it hides a lot beneath that snow. It's the geographic center of New England. Shares a border with Canada. Has both a seacoast and mountains. Massive amounts of forest. Countless lore and legends. Everything from the first alien abduction to the invention of the Teenage Mutant Ninja Turtles happened here. The first American in space was made in New Hampshire. We've got a membership in the Ivy League. J.D. Salinger hid here.

And that's just a thin layer of surface ice. The way to dig deep to uncover the state is exactly how Susanna is doing with this book. By staking out a corner of it. Roping it off like an archeological dig. Digging deep into its history. Its ghosts. Filling in that blank slate for the rest of us.

You're in for some good stories.

> —J.W. Ocker, *USA Today* bestselling and Lowell Thomas- and Edgar Award-winning author of *Poe-Land*, *A Season with the Witch*, *Death and Douglas*, and *The Smashed Man of Dread End*

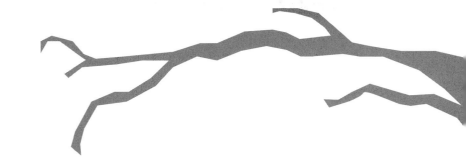

Welcome to Spooky Amherst, New Hampshire!

When you stroll through the quaint, colonial town of Amherst, New Hampshire, you may feel like you've stepped back in time. Well-known for its friendly town commons, stunning Revolutionary War–era homes, scenic country roads, forested trails, family farms, and fields as far as the eye can see, Amherst's rich colonial history seems to linger in the air. In the pages of New Hampshire history, the tales of Amherst unfold like a captivating storybook, filled with brave pioneers and the promise of new beginnings. But did you know that along with all that history... Amherst is also famous for its *ghosts*?

Yes, you read that right: this charming and historic New England town is teeming with spirits! (Which may not be much of a surprise, considering many of the homes and buildings in Amherst are over *300* years old.) Thanks to the preservation that has kept the town's charm intact through the years, Amherst's fascinating past feels alive, and every ghostly footstep and shadowed corner seems to have a story to tell.

Some people have shared their spine-tingling experiences with me. These ghostly encounters often happen when someone moves into a new house or starts renovations, as if the spirits of the past are disturbed by the changes of the modern world. But beyond mere entertainment, ghosts evoke deep emotions in some people. Some believe they are souls trapped between worlds, reaching out from another plane of existence. Others believe ghosts are reminders of our history.

Founded in 1735 by fourteen families descended from King Philip's War veterans, the village of Amherst emerged from the wilderness. Led by Samuel Walton and Samuel Lamson, settlers built their first humble log house on what is now Ponemah Road. The village grew quickly, and they soon built a Congregational church, a minister's home, and a school. Yet, amid the hope of peaceful village life, conflicts loomed from the French and Indian War, casting a shadow of uncertainty and fear. Vigilant and prepared, the settlers kept their muskets close at hand and built a garrison house on Jones Road for protection.

In 1760, Amherst was officially named after Lord Jeffrey Amherst (the same Lord Jeffrey for whom Amherst, Massachusetts, is named). But there is a dark chapter in Lord Amherst's life that must not be overlooked. In 1763, during the Siege of Fort Pitt, he encouraged using blankets infected with smallpox to harm the areas' Indigenous Peoples. This terrible disease took the lives of many, particularly children, and left survivors scarred or blinded for life. Despite this grim discovery, the legacy of Amherst's early settlers lives on, a testament to their courage and perseverance in the face of adversity.

If you're brave enough, please join me on a journey through the shadows of this fascinating colonial town. We'll hear about ghostly wolves in the night and the superstitions of the early settlers. We'll visit the haunted Town Hall, where skeletons were found in the basement. In the center of town, there's an old tavern said to be haunted by ghosts. And don't forget the old jailhouse with its whipping block, where justice was once swift and brutal. The home built on the site of the last public hanging has its own ghostly tales, including a friendly ghost who saved a family from a fire. We'll also explore the doctor's mansion, haunted by the spirits of long-gone patients, and the old farmhouses and lake cottage where ghostly children still play. You will learn about the Abenaki ghostly legends that still echo through the forests along the Souhegan River and Baboosic Lake. And *more*.

But be warned, Dear Reader: These spooky stories are inspired by true accounts and historical events. They are pieced together from personal interviews, family tales, old newspapers, and the historic archives of several libraries—and may just have you sleeping with the lights on!

Whether you believe in ghosts or not, these stories are sure to entertain you and spark discussions. So, if you're seeking thrills or simply looking to embrace the eerie history of the town, these ghostly tales are yours to enjoy and pass on for future generations to come. May you share them with your family and friends, gathered around a crackling fire, by candlelight, or snuggled under the covers with your flashlight in hand.

After all, in Amherst, New Hampshire, you'll find there are ghosts all around us. Ghosts from the past and the present. They exist on the edge of our everyday lives. Let's explore them together!

Town Hall

Tales Passed Down Through the Years

"If a ghost was to appear to me I wouldn't be afraid of him," said Grandmother Brown; "and if some night some of you children see a ghost, you just tell me. I would know, if a ghost came to me, he either wanted help, or came to warn me; and I should just ask him what he wanted. Oh, there's no need of bein' scared of a ghost. If a ghost appeared to a person, the proper words in which to address it were, What, in the name of God, do you want?"

—*What They Say in New England*
by Clifton Johnson, 1897

CHAPTER 1

The Wolves in the Night

Imagine the darkness that enveloped colonial Amherst, with no streetlights to pierce the shadows, only the flicker of candles and the glow of lanterns to ward off the encroaching gloom. The eerie howls of hungry wolves echoing through the night were always just outside the door. They were a chilling symphony of wilderness that kept the settlers awake and made them worry about their families and farm animals.

Wolves, prowling the dense forests that surrounded the settlement, were a constant threat, especially under the cover of night. In the pages of an old book penned by Daniel Secomb, *History of the Town of Amherst* (1883), a settler wrote, "A howling wilderness it was, where no man dwelt."

And one wolf tale has lasted through time.

One summer evening, a young fiddler, merrily returning home from entertaining his fellow townsfolk, found himself pursued by a ravenous wolf pack not far from the Lindabury Orchard. Surrounded and defenseless, he sought refuge atop a large rock. Without a weapon and with nowhere to hide, he opened his instrument case and did what only seemed natural for him.

With nerves of steel, the fiddler serenaded the fearsome creatures with the strains of his fiddle. Talk about a tough audience! At dawn's first light, the wolves dispersed, and the musician escaped unharmed, his music proving to be his salvation. Perhaps the experience inspired a song and added the

much-needed validation the fiddler deserved. After all, it was his musical talent that had kept him alive.

Legend has it that to this day, on windswept nights, one can hear the haunting melody of the fiddler mingling with the mournful cries of the wolves. Listen closely and you may hear their songs.

The Young Lovers' Walk

When the moon is full, beware of the spirit's pull! Do you hear me?

This is an old ghostly New England tale that has been passed down and adapted through the years.

A young Amherst couple in love were strolling in the autumn moonlight through the town commons. Distracted by their conversation, they soon discovered they were in front of the Old Burying Ground behind Town Hall. Noticing how creepy the cemetery looked, they agreed that it would be the perfect place for ghosts. In fun and jest, the young man jumped up onto the rock wall in front of the old cemetery.

He called out as he raised his arms, "All spirits, I command you to rise. Do you hear me? Is anybody there? Rise, I say. Rise!"

As if to answer him, the cold wind began to pick up and howl.

Shivering, the young woman scolded her fiancé to get down and to be respectful of the dead. "Let them rest in peace, or they will haunt you!" she warned. Laughing, he jumped down, kissed her passionately in front of the gate, and asked for forgiveness.

Then, to their horror, they heard the rustling sounds of someone—or *something*—moving in the cemetery. Terrified, they noticed two large white figures slowly roaming from behind the graves, and they were getting closer. For nearly a minute, the couple stood frozen in terror in each other's arms before they realized it was just the village sheep who often grazed in and around the town commons.

Boooooo! Baaahhhh! Baaahhhh!

The Spirit Chair

Benjamin Hastings bought thirteen acres in Amherst and built his home for his beautiful wife, Abigail, and their two daughters in 1830. Tragically, their daughter, Sarah L. Hastings, died at the young age of eleven or twelve on September 12, 1831, just a few months after moving into their new home. In front of the historic house stands an old granite chair steeped in folklore.

The story goes that, with a strong belief in the afterlife, the mourning chair was placed there to symbolize the grief and loss of their loved one. The custom of having the chair supposedly welcomed the spirits back home so they would always have a place to sit and rest. The spirit chair is also a constant symbol of faith and undying love in honor of the loved ones who have passed on. They wanted their loved one to know they would always be remembered and welcome. Even today, such chairs are found in cemeteries, serving as a sanctuary for those to sit and grieve.

Old Superstitions

Within Amherst's town and church death records lie tragic tales of great sorrow and loss. A cursory glance reveals a haunting truth: many souls departed this world prematurely. Diseases such as cholera, diphtheria, measles, dysentery, and whooping-cough swept through the area, leaving behind a trail of grief and despair. The death toll was staggering, claiming lives young and old alike.

Religion and culture played a major role and influenced a superstitious belief system. The tradition of wearing black during mourning served as both shield and shroud—a barrier against spirits that lingered around the corpse.

The widow's black garb of mourning was also considered the correct way for the wearer to share their respect, and it symbolized their grief and protected their privacy. Today, people continue to wear black to wakes and funerals.

Other superstitions served as protection against fears of the unknown. You may have heard of some of these superstitions. (I know of some from my own grandparents and in stories through the years.)

Here are some of the most popular superstitious beliefs to warn and protect us from our impending doom, and some older ones found in *What They Say in New England: A Book of Signs, Sayings, and Superstitions*, published in 1897 by Clifton Johnson:

- If you go over the railroad tracks, cross your fingers.
- If you are passing by a cemetery, hold your breath.
- When someone sneezes, say, "God bless you."
- When a bird flies into the house, death will come.
- To see a "corpse candle" or a small light moving

about with no one holding it means death.
- "The 3 Knocks of Death." If you hear three knocks and no one's there, it means someone you know has died.
- The sounds of a death watch beetle are a warning that death will come.
- If the coffee grounds at the bottom of your cup form a line, there will be a funeral.
- A white moth inside the house, or trying to enter, means death.
- If a dog howls at night when there is illness in the house, it is a bad omen. To neutralize its power, reach under the bed and turn over a shoe.
- To see a tree blooming out of season means death.
- The grass will not grow where a criminal has been hung.
- If you sneeze twice when you first wake up, then news of death will come before night.
- When a dog howls under a window, there will be a death in the household.
- If you spill salt, throw a pinch over your left shoulder to prevent death.
- When a loved one dies, clocks are stopped and

mirrors are covered so the spirit of the deceased does not get trapped.
- At a funeral, if rain falls into the open grave, there will be another death before the end of the year.

Also, in the book *New Hampshire, A Guide to the Granite State*, published in 1938, the descendants of the Puritans were very leery of joy, and if a child woke up in the morning expressing happiness and singing before breakfast, a mother would say, "Hush. Sing before you eat, cry before you sleep."

Have any superstitions been passed down in your family?

The Mysterious Whipping Block on the Amherst Town Green

In the center of Amherst lies a peaceful area known as the town commons or village green. A cherished park dating back to 1868, it was once a grazing ground for villagers' livestock and a gathering point for the local militia. At its core stands a substantial granite block, a relic from a darker past.

When you visit, you will see Town Hall looming just off in the distance behind it. This block, once part of the town's jail, bore witness to the harsh treatment of unruly prisoners. Here, prisoners were shackled and publicly chastised and whipped.

On April 5, 1769, Amherst got a big job: it became the main town for a brand-new county called Hillsborough County with the approval of King George III himself. This meant Amherst was now in charge of running the courts and deciding what happened to people who broke the rules in many nearby towns. His Majesty's Gaol at Amherst (the old term for jail) was quickly built out of logs. This wooden structure was the place where prisoners were held, and it housed the jailkeeper and his family. It *also* had the gallows for public hangings.

Back in those days, if you were up to no good in Amherst, you were in big trouble. People back then thought crime was really bad and a sign of being influenced by evil. They followed strict rules based on religious teachings and old English laws, and punishments were harsh.

Described only as a small log house, many criminals confined in the small, unheated jail suffered or died due to the horrible health conditions and lack of care. The jail also wasn't very secure, and many inmates escaped.

Serious criminals, debtors, adulterers, and the mentally ill were all housed together in this miserable place.

After the state built a new county jail in Manchester and a new era of prison reform and humane practices began, the Amherst jail closed. Much of what could be used was repurposed, including the village green's granite block.

Today, as the sun sets on the town commons, one cannot help but wonder if the ghosts of the past still wander, seeking solace in the shadows in their eternal prison. If there are any ghosts, we certainly understand why they would continue to moan and howl here.

Ghostly Tales

The Friendly Ghost Who Saved the Barnabas David House

Located just a few steps from the center of town is a beautiful brick home. The home was named for Barnabas David, its successful owner who co-founded the whip manufacturing business in Amherst with his brother-in-law, Samuel Melendy.

The mansion was built in 1825 by Attorney Means Jr., who purchased the land on the site of a gruesome event. On a bitter cold Thursday, January 3, 1822, Amherst became the stage for a macabre spectacle etched in New Hampshire history. A crowd numbering over 10,000, braving the winter chill, gathered to witness the grim ending of Daniel Farmer, a Manchester man condemned for the murder of widow Anna Ayer. Daniel's violent outburst stemmed from a drunken dispute over her unborn child and led to a brutal assault and arson (a crime when somebody deliberately sets fire to a building) that claimed Anna's life. After the gallows were dismantled, Attorney Means Jr. purchased the land and built a home for his family.

The house's legacy weaves tales of friendly apparitions and odd events. As new residents moved in and renovations echoed through its halls, some claimed to hear whispers of a spectral woman roaming the shadows. Over the years, the ghost's playful antics amused and baffled the families who dwelled within the home.

As the story goes, children who lived in the home while it was undergoing renovations claimed to have seen a ghost in the night. It was reported that the homeowners did not feel afraid but were very intrigued by it. Another previous resident shared that the friendly ghost supposedly did annoying things like open doors and drawers throughout the house. And yet another reported that furniture was moved around.

There are also accounts of phantom melodies drifting from the kitchen, where a piano played to an invisible audience. Whenever the residents or guests went to see who was playing, no one was there.

Yet, amid these ghostly reveries, a more disturbing event loomed in the house's history. In 1981, flames engulfed the barns and threatened to consume all in their wake. It was then that the kind spirit intervened, rousing the slumbering family from their beds as their sanctuary teetered on the brink of danger and destruction. The ghost managed to wake the daughter up, and she woke the rest of the family up. Thanks to the ghost, the family was able to save their house, but unfortunately, not the barn.

According to an article published on October 25, 1984, in the *Milford Cabinet* by Janet Phelps, that explored some of the history of several homes, the ghost was called a "friendly ghost." The article states that the family of Jeffrey Purtell, who were residing in the home at the time of the article, were told that the ghost moved furniture around. It was wondered if the ghost had set the fire and left after doing so. Or perhaps the ghost had lived in the sheds or barns and, after they burned down, left for good.

The former homeowner shared a theory that the ghost may have once been the loyal driver of one of the barn's old cars that was destroyed in the fire. Could he have awoken the family and saved them from the fire as his last duty before moving on to the next realm? Perhaps it was the spirit of Daniel Farmer, who wanted to make amends for his sins.

As time marched forward, the ghosts that once haunted the halls of the Barnabas David House seemed to fade away. But if you ever decide to take a historic walking tour through Amherst, keep your eyes and ears open. These ghostly tales may very well *still* be haunting the town...

CHAPTER 7

The Haunting of Town Hall

Step into the heart of Amherst, and you'll find Town Hall standing tall and proud on Main Street, overlooking the bustling town commons. Built in 1823, this brick building has heard and seen it all—from the cries of court trials to tears over town bills and taxes.

But as the sun sets and Amherst settles into slumber,

whispers of *another* kind begin to stir within the old walls. Some say Town Hall is haunted, and who can blame them? After all, skeletal remains were discovered in its basement back in 2003, sending shivers down the spines of those who dared to imagine what secrets lay buried beneath. (Learn more in Chapter 25, Skeletons in the Basement.)

One former finance worker often felt the chill of the unknown during her late-night shifts, sensing an eerie presence in the shadows. She dubbed this unseen visitor "Byron," and although his presence unnerved her, she never felt threatened. Instead, it was a subtle feeling of being watched, of never *truly* being alone in the quiet solitude of the night.

The mysterious noises and eerie sensations all seemed to echo from the second floor, where her office was located. Yet, each time she investigated, she found nothing amiss, leaving her with more questions than answers.

"There are two offices on the left-hand side, if you are walking away from the meeting room," she said. "Mine was the closest to the meeting room. The noise came from the storage room behind the meeting room.

Sometimes it would startle me, but the noises didn't scare me. It wasn't a scary feeling. It was just the feeling that I wasn't alone."

So, as you pass by Amherst Town Hall, take a moment to ponder its secrets. Who knows what mysteries lie within its old storied walls? No one knows who haunts the building, or why.

Perhaps the "friendly ghost" just wants to make sure everything is up to code.

The Ghosts in the Green House

Do you believe in ghosts? There is an old house that has had quite a few tales through the years. According to town records, the Amos Green House, originally an expansive eighty-four-acre farm, was constructed in 1770. The Green family, who once resided there, suffered significant hardships and losses before selling the farm. Despite changes in ownership over the years, the stately colonial-style residence has stood the test of time, along with several ghost stories.

Upon moving into the house in 2015, Lisa encountered a series of perplexing occurrences that left her bewildered. On multiple occasions, she awoke to discover that a ball or stuffed animal had mysteriously appeared beside her bed. Another puzzling incident unfolded one morning as Lisa sat sipping her coffee and perusing the newspaper. Out of nowhere, Lisa got a sudden urge to investigate the fireplace's small ash cubby. To her surprise, she found a trove of old paper dolls inside the fireplace.

"It was utterly random. I can't explain why I felt compelled to reach in, but there they were," Lisa recounted, noting that she has since safeguarded the paper dolls in a special container.

These odd events prompted Lisa to delve into the history of her home. She learned from a previous owner that children had reported sightings of a ghostly child within its walls.

According to Tom Wilkins, his grandfather, Harold Wilkins Jr., (a descendant of the founding family of Rev. Daniel Wilkins) shared with him a ghostly tale during his teenage years while they tended to the lots and pruned trees near the Amos Green House.

One day, many years ago, when the Amos Green farm was known as the Towne farm, workers reported encountering a ghostly presence. As they stacked hay bales in the barn, they were startled by the appearance of a young girl who expressed concern about her toys being lost in a fire. Although Tom's grandfather could not explain why, the workers were convinced the girl was a ghost.

David and Susan, a couple who resided in the Amos Green House from 1996 to 2015, said their purchase agreement included mention of a ghost sighting on the property. "We were informed that only children could see it," David recalled. Susan added that the previous owner, Martha, relayed stories of her five children encountering the apparition of a young boy, which had made them a little hesitant before their move.

"I remember thinking, should we do this?" Susan added. In the end, they loved the home and decided to move in. But it wasn't long before their family also experienced peculiar occurrences, particularly when their young son was playing in the living room. "All of a sudden," Susan recounted, "he sat up straight and was staring in the corner. He was spooked, and he wouldn't move." She explained how her son's eyes followed something all through the room, and how he even talked to this unseen person for thirty seconds.

One day, former residents visited Susan and David. They were curious about changes made to the home. In conversation, they brought up the topic of the ghost, sharing it was supposedly the spirit of their deceased brother, although he hadn't died in the house but rather in Mont Vernon.

Susan's other son claimed to have encountered an apparition, waking one night to the sight of a woman in a white nightgown at the foot of his bed. Another unsettling incident involved a friend visiting while the family was away. She heard the back door opening and closing and footsteps, despite being alone in the house. (Talk about spooky!)

Later, a contractor was alone in the house while refinishing the upstairs floors when he discovered a child's footprint on the threshold... even though there were no children anywhere in sight. "He was convinced the house was haunted," Susan said.

Despite her family's many eerie experiences at the Amos Green House, Susan said she never had a feeling there was anything bad. She just sometimes sensed someone was there.

A psychic who once visited the home told Susan there was a Native American spirit in the barn and an old man living on the third floor. Susan said she was *convinced* it was Amos.

On the day Susan moved out, she had a powerful experience. "I lived there for seventeen years. I was saying goodbye. I was leaving out the door, and I looked back, and I saw hundreds of orbs. They looked like fireflies. It gave me chills, and I felt like they were also saying goodbye."

Ghosts in the Doctor's Mansion

This tale originates from the records of the Amherst Historical Society and several interviews. The Dr. Matthias Spalding mansion is known not only for its architectural grandeur but also for the legacy of its illustrious former residents.

Constructed in 1770, the stately abode was initially home to Robert and Samuel Stewart. Later, the home was expanded upon by Samuel Dana, an esteemed attorney who eventually earned the role of Judge of Hillsborough County Probate. Yet, it is Dr. Matthias

Spalding who gave the mansion the most significance, thanks to his efforts in smallpox eradication and medical care in the community.

But Dr. Spalding's legacy is not the *only* lingering presence in the halls of the mansion. According to Sue, who lived there from 1991 to 2006, the spirit of a mischievous young girl is said to wander its corridors. Despite many eerie occurrences, Sue maintained a friendly relationship with the ghostly inhabitant. When strange things happened, like mysteriously reappearing watches and misplaced jewelry, Sue knew they were just the playful antics of the spectral child.

Sue and her husband had bought the house from a lady named Carol, who'd told her all about the ghost. She said there had been a little girl who had died in one of the original front bedrooms. Carol claimed that this little girl ghost would look out the windows, and that she had seen her multiple times. To Sue's relief, Carol said the child ghost was friendly and not to be feared.

Over the next few months, there were interesting noises and some odd placement of things. Sue felt the girl's presence multiple times and even thought she caught a glimpse of her. "Basically, I acknowledged her, and we got along just fine," Sue explained. "There were several times when I couldn't find something and would hunt and hunt for it, and then magically, it would show up in front of me. I always felt that the little girl had something to do with the item showing up."

Then Sue began to lose her watches. This was during the time before cell phones. Sue would have a watch for a month or so, and then, for some mysterious reason, it would disappear. "I only wore inexpensive watches," Sue said, "so I would just go out and buy another one. This happened at least ten times over a period of several years. Then I got an expensive watch that I really liked, and I really tried to keep track of it. Of course, it disappeared, too. At this point, I was getting a little exasperated. So, one day I went into the bedroom where I kept my jewelry and watches, and I said out loud, 'Okay, enough is enough! Give me back my watches!'

"The next morning, when I got up and went to the room, all ten watches were lined up on the bed! I knew it was the little girl ghost who had taken them. I felt that ghosts probably have some fascination with time, and I thanked her profusely. That is a true story," Sue said.

Sue explained there were a few other times where she lost a piece of jewelry and was unable to find it. "I would ask her to bring it back, and she always did. When we were moving out of the house, I found a piece of jewelry in plain sight that I didn't even know I had lost."

One night, the family was in the living room. Suddenly, they heard a child screaming! The screams were coming from the back door. When they opened the door, it stopped, and no one was there.

Sue's daughter, Becca, shared a chilling encounter with a somber ghost standing at the foot of her bed. Late one night, Becca said she couldn't sleep. Something made her look toward the bottom of her bed. Standing there was a bald-headed man wearing spectacles.

"I see a figure standing over me. He was an older gentleman wearing a dark suit with spectacles on, and he was holding a bouquet of flowers. He looked so sad. I pulled the covers over my head." Becca said when she looked again, he was gone.

Another resident, Kate, described a peculiar phenomenon of raindrops falling from a dry ceiling. "I would go to turn on the light in the library or dining room, and there would be raindrops coming down only from the entryway." She went on to explain there was no leak or puddle, and that this had happened several times.

A family friend named Shannon house-sat for them one night while they were out of town. She was trying to go to sleep when—from the other side of the house—she suddenly heard the door open and shut. When Shannon heard footsteps, she assumed it was another friend stopping by, but when she went downstairs to investigate, no one was there! Then, from where she had just been, she heard the door to the guest room slam shut and footsteps. She immediately left.

The ghostly experiences have happened less and less through the years. Now, new memories are being made to fill this grand home. However, a family member visiting the house reported hearing a door open and shut upstairs while he was eating lunch in the kitchen. And yet, when he went to look ... no one was upstairs. He chuckled and said that it must have been the ghost. Then he happily went back to eating his sandwich.

Despite these ghostly occurrences, the mansion continues to be a cherished home. The spirit of Dr. Spalding himself, revered for his dedication to his community, remains a lasting presence in the history of Amherst.

The Haunted History of the Aaron Lawrence House

Here is an intriguing tale of the Aaron Lawrence House, a charming abode built in 1846 by the skilled hands of Captain Daniel Hartshorn, a renowned foundry owner. For Jeanne and her husband, Will, residing in this historic dwelling on School Street has been a forty-year journey filled with peculiar occurrences and spectral encounters.

They bought the house when Will was stationed at Hanscom Air Force Base in 1983. From the moment they crossed the threshold, the Lawrence House seemed to harbor secrets of its own. Mysterious footsteps echoed through its halls, and both children and pets would fix their gaze on unseen entities drifting through the dining room. Every so often, they would hear and see the dining room door inexplicably unlatch and swing open, as if beckoning to some unseen visitor.

Despite the odd occurrences, Jeanne never felt fear, always sensing a friendly presence within the walls of their home. Even family guests encountered the house's spectral quirks. One night, Jeanne's mother-in-law fell asleep with her glasses on. When she awoke the next morning without her glasses, she asked Jeanne if she'd come in to take them off—but she hadn't.

When duty called them away, Jeanne and Will entrusted their beloved home to renters, the local high school principal and his family. True to form, the new occupants soon found themselves startled by unexplained noises and eerie sensations, prompting an amusing encounter with local law enforcement. According to Jeanne, the principal called the police because he and his family heard someone walking about and thought someone was in the house.

"I forgot to tell them the house was haunted," Jeanne added with a chuckle.

Returning home, Jeanne took note of the broken latch on the dining room door, a minor inconvenience that seemed to mark the end of the ghostly escapades. Yet, as if to remind them of its presence, the house found a new way to make itself known—a silent clock, dormant for years, suddenly chimed all on its own, ringing out through the living room with no visible cause.

"I hate ticking clocks, and the clock does not have a pendulum, and it hadn't been wound in years. Out of the blue, it just started bonging on its own at random times." Jeanne had recently joined the school board and was determined to uncover the home's history. She delved into the life of Aaron Lawrence, a kind merchant whose philanthropic endeavors left a positive mark on the community.

"He was generous, and he gave money to be distributed to the schools. A friend and I looked into the funds, and they had not been used in thirty years," Jeanne said.

Inspired by his legacy, Jeanne took action to bring back Lawrence's gifts to the schools and created a fund for teachers in his honor. The ghostly disturbances ceased, and the household became peaceful.

The Ghost of the Spinster

The Timothy & Hannah Jones House stands within the village of Amherst and dates back to 1860, as documented by the records of the Historical Society. Over time, it became intertwined with the house behind it.

Stacey's family moved into the residence in 2000, and she recalled the early days were filled with renovations. Feelings of an eerie presence made itself known when their young daughter began waking in the night and claiming that someone was in her room.

Strange noises echoed through the halls, and doors creaked open and shut.

At first, Stacey dismissed the disturbances as quirks of an old home. That is, until one fateful evening. While they were eating dinner, Stacey lit a candle in a glass vase. All of a sudden, the flame jumped—and the entire wall caught fire! Luckily, they had an extinguisher and put the fire out. Not even a month later, however, *another* candle caught fire on the second floor. Once again, they were able to react quickly and put the fire out. From that day on, Stacey got rid of the candles and bought battery-operated candles instead. Not long after, to their horror, they had a chimney fire from the wood stove. Fortunately, yet again, they were able to get the fire out.

When the furnace erupted into flames—now the *fourth* fire in the home—the family's resilience wavered. Their daughter's playroom was in ruin, consumed by soot and despair. "Every toy, book, and stuffed animal had to be thrown out," Stacey said. "We thought this was very bad luck. It was very scary."

As their daughter's unease intensified, visions of an elderly specter began to haunt her dreams. Stacey's daughter became very scared and told her an old woman stood at the foot of her bed. Stacey was skeptical and brushed off these encounters. But a chance meeting with a visiting medium (a person with a gift for sensing spirit energy) revealed a chilling truth. The medium told Stacey there was an old woman spinster spirit in her house, and that she was uncomfortable having Stacey's daughter in the house. The medium said the old woman did not mean any harm, but that she was responsible for the fires to scare them out of her space.

Determined to reclaim their sanctuary, Stacey enlisted the aid of the medium and a circle of close friends for a cleansing ceremony. With sage and bells, they purged the lingering presence, bidding the ghost farewell, and restoring peace to the home.

The ghost never returned.

CHAPTER 12

The Ghosts of the John Watson Tavern

In the center of town stands a majestic historic home built in 1795 for Mr. John Watson, a saddler turned tavern keeper. Once known as Boylston Corner, this respected abode holds within its walls a tapestry of history.

Transformed from a bustling tavern to a cherished family residence, the old home is said to harbor more than just memories of its former glory.

A previous owner shared her ghostly encounters, recounting sightings of colonial-era apparitions that graced the halls. Her daughter, on two separate occasions, bore witness to the spectral forms of young girls.

The first time, her daughter saw the ghost of a little girl with curly hair in a colonial dress standing in the dining room, watching the family in the kitchen. The same daughter awoke one night to see a second teenage girl holding flowers. The body of the ghost was facing the window, but her face was turned, and she was looking toward her.

Even craftsmen working within the home have felt the chilling touch of the supernatural. One witness described an encounter with a ghostly figure clad in formal attire. "We were having our floors refinished, and the man doing them saw a little man dressed in a tuxedo staring at him. The worker said he would never come back to do work on our house."

Another time the family witnessed an unusual event was in the kitchen. One evening after dinner, the owner's daughter's long ponytail flew up in the air for no reason. It was as if someone had flicked her hair up in the air. "We all saw it! It was like a breeze, but no windows or doors were open."

The owner also reported that she would randomly smell perfume in her bedroom. The mysterious scent could not be located and would soon fade away.

Despite having ghostly residents, the family never felt afraid in their home.

As the years marched on, the old tavern has become a home filled with happy memories.

CHAPTER 13

The Ghost in Martin's House

This tale comes from Will, a lifelong resident of Amherst, who recalls a chilling encounter at the old Martin family home. The old farmhouse was nestled on a quiet road called Fellow's Farm off Chestnut Hill.

Years ago, Will found himself house-sitting and caring for the family dog while they were away. Upon entering the colonial home, he noticed the layout: the dining room to the left, the living room to the right, and straight ahead, the staircase leading upstairs. On the first night, for reasons he couldn't explain, Will closed the door to the dining room, wrestling with its warped thumb latch.

The next morning, to his surprise, Will discovered the door wide open. The same thing happened the following two nights, even though Will placed a chair in front of the door to block it from opening. Feeling perplexed rather than frightened, Will persisted. He closed the door.

Then, in the dead of night, the unmistakable sound of footsteps ascending the stairs, echoing through the silent house, jolted him awake. Even the dog reacted, confirming that he wasn't alone in his perception. The footsteps seemed to continue into another bedroom across the hall. Will looked and no one was there. However, he had the unsettling sensation he was being watched.

Eventually, the Martin family relocated, and the old house was torn down to make way for a modern one. But for Will, the eerie experiences in that old home haunt him to this day.

The Reasons Why Karen & Joe Called Ghost Hunters

In 1884, the Whiting Farmhouse was erected by Benjamin Billings Whiting and his family. It started as a bustling farm, spanning 506 acres, but as time passed, the land was gradually sold off, giving way to a neighborhood of homes. Through the years, the farmhouse and barn stood firm along with a few ghostly inhabitants.

Karen and Joe became the caretakers of this historic home in 2005. For Joe, a skeptic turned believer, the presence of ghosts became an undeniable reality.

Joe stated that he never believed in ghosts until they moved into their house.

"I just never thought ghosts were a real thing, but now I believe. Once you live with it, you realize there is definitely something out there," Joe said. However, despite the eerie occurrences, fear found no place in their hearts. The couple poured their love into the house, restoring it with much care and dedication.

The first revelation of the house's haunted history came as a surprise during the closing. The former owner casually mentioned a ghost named Penelope, seen by her in a white bonnet and green dress. Soon after settling in, Karen and Joe's encounters with the supernatural began.

Strange events plagued their home: sudden drops in temperature, mysterious footsteps, swinging chandeliers, and unexplained electrical malfunctions. Even the lights flickered at will, defying all attempts at rational explanation. Their experiences reached a peak during a visit from a friend, when the entire house plunged into darkness at the mention of ghosts.

Despite efforts to fix the home's electrical problems, the occurrences persisted, leaving the couple feeling unsettled. Joe called the electrician and was told there was no explanation for what was going on in the house.

One night, Karen came home to a dark house. She called Joe as she went through the mudroom to turn on the light. The moment her fingers touched the switch, the whole switch blew off the wall and broke the screws right in half!

Panicked, Joe told Karen to call the fire department. When they arrived, Karen learned the fire chief was an electrician, too. Karen explained the strange situation. She said they had just had the electrical done and the switch was brand new. The fire chief replied that he had never seen anything like it. "The fire chief told me, well, you know this house is haunted," Karen said.

Some time later, Karen encountered the ghostly figure of a woman in a bonnet, staring back at her from an antique mirror. Their bedroom became a hotspot for paranormal activity, with shadows darting in the darkness and strange figures appearing in doorways.

Still, despite many chilling encounters in the house, there were also moments of unexpected assistance. Karen recalled a near fall down the stairs, only to be steadied by an invisible hand. The couple reported other odd things. Mysterious sulfuric odors and unexplained gusts of wind filled the air, leaving the couple unnerved. Even their skeptical friend was convinced after a saltshaker mysteriously flew across the room.

Desperate for answers, Karen and Joe enlisted the help of professional ghost hunters. Their investigations unearthed eerie recordings of ghostly voices, confirming the presence of two spirits—a man and a woman—haunting their home.

Thankfully, since Karen and Joe finished their renovations, the spooky activity has calmed down. To this day, they remain very happy in their home with their beloved dogs . . . and the ghosts.

The Nightly Rattlings of Mr. Pesterfield

Another intriguing ghost story passed down through the years is shared from the Upper Flanders area, which was the center of town until 1755. The house in question was built in 1762 and once included seventy acres of farmland.

Fast forward to the early twentieth century, and the house became the residence of Mr. John Pesterfield and his wife, Kate, who took up residence in 1906. Mr. Pesterfield was rumored to dabble in bootlegging (the illegal making and selling of alcohol) and hunting to supplement their income. After they died years later, the house changed hands multiple times. Yet, it wasn't until the early 1980s that tales of Mr. Pesterfield's spectral presence emerged. During renovations, one of the daughters of a residing family supposedly encountered Mr. Pesterfield himself, declaring his identity from beyond the grave.

Mysterious movements of objects, inexplicable noises, and sightings of Mr. Pesterfield rattled the nerves of those who dwelled within. One eerie tale recounted a rocking chair swaying of its own accord. A neighbor told a story of a shotgun the family found one morning on the kitchen table...even though it had been mounted on the wall the night before. (Creepier still is the fact that this happened on more than one occasion!)

In an article published in the *Milford Cabinet* in 1998, "Grisly Tale of Two Houses: The Ghost of Mack Hill Road," neighbors reminisced about Mr. Pesterfield's life. They remembered him as an avid hunter and a recluse.

Jo-Ellen, a former resident, shared her own experiences with Mr. Pesterfield. She and her husband bought their home on December 23, 1986, when she was nine months pregnant with her second child. She reports that she had strange feelings about the home from the very start. While standing in the kitchen, Jo-Ellen once felt a cold breeze. When she asked her husband if he felt it, too, he answered no. She didn't think much of it. Then, when they were closing on the house, their realtor shared a rumor of a friendly spirit in the house.

"That's when I knew the breeze I'd felt was something," Jo-Ellen said. She had trouble sleeping and would often hear footsteps go by the bedroom and down the stairs to the first floor every night. "I would tell my husband, and he would shrug it off. Not until after I had the baby and we were out with friends did I find out he heard it too and didn't want to frighten me," Jo-Ellen said.

Another day, when Jo-Ellen and her two-year-old son were having lunch in the kitchen and the baby was up taking a nap, her son started talking to someone and showing them a potato chip, explaining what it was. "I asked him who he was talking to, and he said the nice man that visits me sometimes." Her son described the tall man as wearing a big hat and that his name was John.

She also said she would hear a baby crying, but it wasn't hers. Despite the eerie occurrences, Jo-Ellen harbored no fear, feeling instead a sense of protection coming from the ghostly presence.

The hauntings ended around 1990, when some friends came to visit. The friend told Jo-Ellen that the ghost came to them during the night, sat down on the bed, and "scared the bejesus out of him." But in an unexpected twist, their friend's new wife ... happened to be a witch.

Jo-Ellen shared, "I had to go out of the house and do errands, and when I came back, my house smelled like incense. When I asked her what she was doing, she told me she was freeing the spirits of the house. She said there was a baby, a grandmother, and a man. From that day on, I never heard the ghosts again. I was actually kind of sad."

The Mischievous Ghost at the Blunt House

In 1996, Susan and her family moved into the John Blunt House on Old Jailhouse Road. Town records trace its origins to 1840, yet the true design of this Greek Revival vernacular-style home remains a mystery. Susan explained that the house is actually two houses put together, and they aren't sure which one was built first. But what they *are* sure of is the story of a ghost haunting the house.

As Susan settled into her new home, she soon found herself experiencing something beyond explanation.

Like clockwork on many nights, at the witching hour of 3:00 a.m., the heavy metal screen before the fireplace would topple over, accompanied by the eerie sound of the kitchen timer sharply ringing in the night. These unexplained events jolted Susan from her slumber, leaving her exhausted and searching for answers. How could these things happen at the same time and on their own? To add to the mystery, Susan's belongings, like her purse, would mysteriously disappear, only to turn up in odd places.

During her husband's absence on a business trip, Susan's young son confided in her about a chilling encounter. He claimed to have glimpsed a shadowy figure in his closet, despite Susan's assurance that she had not ventured into his room that night. The revelation sent shivers down Susan's spine as she grappled with the unsettling presence lurking within their home.

What was trying to get her attention? And what did they want?

Fortunately, the previous owner presented Susan with a collection of old photographs depicting his grandmother cradling her beloved cat. Feeling it might improve the energy of the home, Susan carefully framed these mementos and put them on display around the house.

"When we finished the renovations, it all died down, and all the spooky things stopped. I always felt it was kind of an approval," Susan mused. A sense of calm settled over the John Blunt House, and nothing ghostly has happened since.

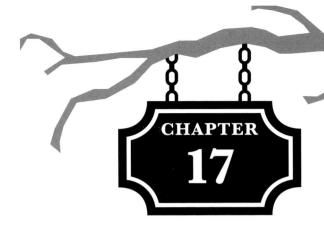

The Ghost of Converse Farm

The Converse Farm is a lasting example of Amherst's rich history and earliest settlers. Once belonging to Robert Converse, a Revolutionary War veteran, the farm eventually evolved into a duplex accompanied by various outbuildings, including a garage, sheds, and a spacious barn.

Clint and his family called this historic homestead their own from 2007 to 2015. During these years, his family had a friendly ghostly experience involving his daughter, Alexis, and their cat.

Alexis even painted a vivid picture of her ghostly companion, whom she called "Charlotte." She described Charlotte as having blonde hair styled in two braids adorned with delicate pink ribbons, her attire a charming mix of vintage flair and whimsy.

Charlotte was always full of laughter and mischief, Alexis reminisced, and she liked to play with dolls. Though Alexis mostly interacted with Charlotte in her bedroom, she sometimes saw her in the hall or playing peekaboo behind the staircase railings or upstairs hallway. "Occasionally, I would see Charlotte in our front living room, warming herself by the fireplace that was no longer functional. If she wanted to play a game, it was always ring around the rosy. And infrequently, we would play tag among these three places, but mostly it was just dolls in my bedroom."

Alexis knew that Charlotte was no ordinary playmate. To Alexis, Charlotte appeared as flesh and blood, yet somehow, the ghostly girl cast a translucent aura over her surroundings, and her touch was chilling to the bone.

"Her hands were always so cold," Alexis said.

Despite the girls' animated interactions, Alexis's parents could never detect Charlotte's spectral presence. "They couldn't see her," Alexis lamented. "My dad would amuse me sometimes and ask me how Charlotte was if I'd mentioned I was playing with her, and she would usually reply, 'I'm cold' or 'I'm hungry.' Or she would panic and say it was time to go and she'd disappear."

As Alexis entered her teenage years, Charlotte's visits dwindled. Yet, Alexis would occasionally glimpse her from the attic window. Then, Charlotte's appearances eventually ceased altogether.

In addition to Charlotte, Clint recalled peculiar behavior from their family cat, who seemed fixated on unseen entities lurking in the shadows. After doing some research, Clint unearthed a tragic tale of a girl named Charlotte, who had succumbed to cholera in the early nineteenth century. Though she hadn't died within the farmhouse's walls, it seemed her presence still lingered in the place she once called home.

CHAPTER 18

Children of the Lake

Baboosic Lake is the largest body of water in Amherst. Formed over 10,000 years ago by ancient glaciers and nourished by babbling brooks and springs, families have flocked to vacation and relax in its tranquil waters for generations. But beware, for among the cozy cottages and serene sparkling water lurks several ghostly tales.

Sadly, several deaths have occurred in the depths of Baboosic Lake. Over the years, ghostly cries and voices have been reported. Not far from the town beach stands a haunted vacation rental. Built in the 1940s alongside a cluster of charming cottages, this house has a story to tell.

Lisa and her husband, Keith, rented the cottage on Baboosic Lake with their two small children in 2005 for a summer family reunion and anniversary celebration. On the first night of their stay, Lisa found herself alone with the children, as Keith was called away for work. After a day filled with laughter and splashing in the cool lake water, Lisa tucked her children into bed,

snuggling close for warmth and comfort. But as the night deepened, a sudden chill swept through the air. Lisa awoke with a start, her senses tingling with the unmistakable feeling of an unseen presence lingering in the shadows.

"I just felt like something was there, and I sat up in the darkness. I remember having such a feeling of dread. I felt like someone was at the bottom of the bed staring at us, but nothing was there." For a while, Lisa remained awake, her senses on high alert until the feeling gradually faded, allowing her to drift back to sleep.

The following night, Keith returned. His arrival brought Lisa a sense of reassurance, and everyone settled contentedly into bed. But as midnight approached, Keith was startled awake by the sound of tiny footsteps and the jarring sight of a child standing by the bed.

"I thought I saw my son," Keith said. "I reached out to grab him, but he ducked and went under the bed. When I got up to look, though, nothing was under there. I checked on the kids, and they both were asleep."

As the nights passed, the strange occurrences

continued. Lisa started to hear phantom coos echoing through the baby monitor, only to find her children sleeping soundly in their cribs.

Baffled and unsettled, Lisa and Keith came to a haunting realization: the cottage had to be haunted. They couldn't help but wonder if these ghostly visitors were souls lost to the depths of the lake, returning to their cherished home in the afterlife.

Hopefully, the children of the lake have found their peace in the arms of their mother's love.

Indigenous Folklore

Once upon a time, in the land of Amherst's ancient forests and rolling hills, lived the Abenaki people, known as the "Dawn Land People" or the "People of the Dawn." These Indigenous people, speaking the Algonquian tongue, thrived across the expanse of New England. They roamed the woodlands, traded with neighboring tribes, and shared their wisdom with the settlers.

As Michael J. Caduto and Joseph Bruchac discussed in their 1994 book, *Keepers of the Night*, the Abenaki presence is important to the area's history. Their stories shared their beliefs in the spirits of the animals and elements. Through the art of storytelling, they would weave a tale by fire light to entertain and teach lessons to their children.

The Lake Spirits

For those looking for an ancient tale pertaining to Baboosic Lake, listen closely. In the enchanting tapestry of Abenaki folklore, there is the ever-present spirit of the loon. This creature emerges as a mystical messenger known as the "spirit bird" or the "magic bird." With its haunting calls that drift across the waters and its graceful dives beneath the surface, the loon is said to call out warnings to all. In the language of the Abenaki people, the loon is known as Medawisla or Medawihla, a name whispered softly as muh-dah-wee-lah, according to *Abenaki Legends, Myths, and Stories* by Laura Redish and Orrin Lewis.

As you listen for the ethereal song of the lovely loon echoing over Baboosic Lake, heed its message with safety and care. The song is a warning to take care of the lake and each other. Perhaps the loon's song is simply telling us to let the magical powers of the water heal us and to rest. Their call is a reminder that we are always connected to the spirit world. In its song, may we find comfort knowing we are never truly alone.

But beware, dear friends, for lurking in the depths of Baboosic Lake is the mighty Tatoskok, the underwater horned serpent. With a name that rolls off the tongue as tah-toh-skog, this ancient guardian watches over the sacred waters. Slithering silently along the lake's edge, Tatoskok seeks out punishment and revenge on those who disrespect the water.

So, as you venture forth to explore the wonders of Baboosic Lake, remember the lessons of the loon and the warnings of Tatoskok. Clean up after yourselves, be kind to one another, and cherish the beauty of this magical realm we share. For in the heart of nature's embrace, we find not only peace and healing but also the timeless wisdom of the spirits that dwell within.

Remember, Baboosic Lake is a special place for us all to enjoy.

Tatoskok is watching over the lake. Always.

CHAPTER 20

The River Spirits

In Amherst history, the common area for fishing and hunting has always been along the banks of the Skowohigan or Zawhigan River, which is now known as the Souhegan River ("meaning the waiting and watching place of the Indians," according to Henry Lorne Masta in his book, *Abenaki Indian Legends, Grammar, and Place Names*. The Souhegan River meanders through the wooded areas in a west-east direction of the southern part of the town, and it continues to provide a tranquil place for residents to connect with nature.

The Souhegan River is also named for the tribe (who were part of the Abenaki) who inhabited the area, hunted and fished, and planted their crops along its shore. According to Daniel Secomb in his book *History of the Town of Amherst*, "it is said that skeletons, supposed to be those of [Indigenous Peoples], have been washed from their graves on the banks of the Souhegan."

There is folklore pertaining to river spirits living here along the wooded shores. The Manogemasak is pronounced mah-nawn-guh-mah-sock, according to Laura Redish and Orrin Lewis. The legend of these little river elves is that they protect and live along the riverbanks. They enjoy creating mischief with harmless pranks such as ripping fishing nets, stealing snacks or objects (don't go skinny-dipping; they will take your clothes), and capsizing canoes. If you are fishing along the Souhegan River, stay humble and respectful. Don't make a lot of noise. The elves don't like that. Easily irritated by loud disturbances, you don't want to experience their wrath!

Some legends say the elves have been known to grant wishes from time to time, but consider yourself warned. These tiny river dwellers are not to be trusted, for they always have their own interests at heart.

So, dear readers, if you find yourself by the banks of the Souhegan River, remember to offer a word of thanks or a small token of gratitude to these mystical spirits. If you have a kind and genuine heart, they will know and protect you.

But be on guard!

The Swamp Woman

Here is a tale as old as the whispering winds. Deep within the murky depths of the bog or swamp lurks the haunting legend of the Swamp Woman, a ghostly figure who weeps in sorrow.

According to Abenaki legend, a beautiful, crying ghost lives deep in the bog or swamp. Anyone who hears her and tries to follow the sound of her wails may be lost forever. Through the years, her story has been told as a warning to children to not wander away or venture into the swamp alone, or they will be lost forever in her ghostly embrace. The Swamp Woman is also known as a fierce protector of the area and its animals, and she will punish anyone who harms the creatures of this land. She also has the ability to shapeshift into various creatures, along with the power to disappear into the mist and fog.

Whispers from the trees warn that the Swamp Woman is quite the sneaky spirit, deliberately leading children to their early demise. Some say the spirit is the heartbroken soul of a grieving mother who calls out for children to join her. The children die when her cold, ghostly hands grasp theirs, and they are doomed to live with her in the afterworld.

But fear not, for you hold the power to evade her curse. Never, ever, venture into the bog, marsh, or swamp during the fog, and *especially* do not go there after dark. Please be respectful of these beautiful places and take care of the environment.

If you hear the haunting cries of the Swamp Woman, run—and don't dare look back. For in the forest, there are secrets best left undisturbed.

The Spirit of Joe English

During the early days of the settlement, the Souhegan River was the place where Indigenous Peoples from various tribes hunted for game. One of the hunters who sometimes visited Amherst was a scout and hunting guide named Joe English by the settlers.

In his book, *The History of Manchester,* published in 1856, C.E. Potter wrote that Joe English was known for his great friendship with the English settlers. Today, Joe English is a legend in this area for being a Native American who bravely risked his life. Joe English had the reputation for being a cunning hunter and a helpful guide. Unfortunately, not everyone was happy about Joe's friendships with the settlers. And in the end, he was said to have made many enemies . . .

One tale has Joe running for his life from his enemies through the hills of Amherst and southern New Boston. They chased him through the woods and up a steep hill. As Joe came upon the edge of a cliff, he leaped behind a jutting rock. His enemies ran off the rocky cliff and fell to their deaths, where they became food for the hungry wolves.

Later, Joe English settled down and started a family in Dunstable (now known as the Nashua area). Eventually, his enemies did catch up to him. Daniel Secomb wrote that Joe English died from the blows of a tomahawk and, "His death was lamented as a public loss."

For his bravery and friendship, the spirit of Joe English lives on in the trails of the Joe English Reservation. Legend has it that during the twilight hour on the night of the full moon, you may still hear in the distance the ardent battle cry of Joe English and his chasers in the wind.

Rev. Daniel Wilkins Table Grave

Graves of the Past

Pauper's Cemetery

Hidden beyond the busy roads of Route 101A and Route 122 (also known as Ponemah Road) in Amherst is a small cemetery called Pauper's Cemetery.

Surrounded by pine trees and an old white fence, the grave is the resting place for the town's poor citizens. In 1831, Amherst bought a big farm to help people in need, and by 1840, part of it became a special graveyard for the poor.

The cemetery shows how the town cared for its struggling members so long ago. Although the identities of those buried there are unknown, the cemetery stands as a testament to the town's efforts to care for its struggling members.

They are remembered, always.

(But if you decide to visit Pauper's Cemetery, beware. It is surrounded by poison ivy.)

CHAPTER 24

The Old Burying Ground

Also known as the Amherst Old Town Cemetery, the Old Burying Ground is said to be one of the oldest public burial grounds in the state of New Hampshire, with graves dating back to 1736. (That's almost 300 years!) As you walk through the cemetery, notice how the gravestones feature carvings of winged skulls, angels, urns, and willow trees. Many of Amherst's founding settlers are buried here. Among the old graves are the following haunting epitaphs to ponder.

"Behold all you that now pass by.
As you are now so was I
As I am now so must you be,
Prepare for Death and follow me."

—Lt. Joseph Prince 1789,
first settler in Amherst and from Salem, MA

"Like as the Vernal flower
This Youth did once appear;
But death like an untimely frost
Laid her in silence here."

—Sally Eaton 1803—in her fifteenth year of life

"The Sweet Remembrance of the Just
Shall Flourish When He Sleep in Dust."

—Rev. Daniel Wilkins, 1783
Amherst's first minister, a founding
leader, and "Father of the Town"

Skeletons in the Basement

In a tale reminiscent of Sherlock Holmes, Nancy Drew, or Scooby Doo, Amherst has a mystery that includes skeletons in the basement. In 2003, a most gruesome discovery brought the much-needed renovations of Town Hall to a complete stop. A skull and part of a well-preserved skeleton were discovered under a corner of the foundation by the construction crew. As required by state law, the office of the coroner was called. Scientists would help solve this mystery.

Archaeologists Kathleen Wheeler, PhD, and

Alexandra Chan, PhD, from Portsmouth, New Hampshire, determined the bones belonged to an adult female between the ages of twenty and twenty-nine of African descent, and a young child around three to five years of age. Both appeared to have lived around 1740–1774. Scientific and historical research was done in the hopes of learning the identity of the young woman and child.

And there were more. During the dig, the scientists revealed other skeletal remains. They recovered a molar tooth, two skull fragments, and five pieces of unidentifiable bones that belonged to another individual. In 2007, after careful studies, the remains were reburied in "a dignified manner" in a cemetery near where they were discovered. It is important to share that the Old Town Cemetery is right behind Town Hall. So, why weren't these individuals buried in the cemetery?

According to old burial customs during the colonial era, witches and others possessed by the devil could not be buried in sacred ground, so they were buried outside the walls of the cemetery.

The haunting questions remain: Who *was* this young woman? Who was the child by her side? Who were the others? How did they get there? What other secrets does the old, historic town hold? After all of this time, we may never know.

May they rest in peace.

A Ghostly Goodbye

Thank you for reading these tales. This book started because of a few weird things that happened. First, our bedroom television turned on in the middle of the night. Then, it happened again in our daughter's room. Then, another night, the TV turned on in the living room. A neighbor believed her home to be haunted by a child. Another neighbor's old barn light kept turning on mysteriously all by itself. These strange things made me wonder: *What if?* This little yet powerful question led to more questions. To my delight, more neighbors wanted to tell their stories.

I hope you will try your hand at telling some of these stories or sharing your own stories with others, so they will be remembered. Storytelling is a fun way to connect, build communication skills, and encourage imagination. It is a way to share and discuss your thoughts and beliefs with others. Telling historic and ghostly tales is one way you can help keep the past alive and inspire a love for learning. You can learn more great stories from our history and culture by joining the Historical Society and visiting your local library.

And there, you will realize that anything is possible.

Community Spirit Endures at the Amherst Congregational Church

You Still Haunt Me

By Susanna Hargreaves

Sometimes I search the shadows,
For the memories seem to linger
just here and there.
During the briefest moments,
a cold breeze will softly blow—
or was it you who caressed my hair?
Then just as simply,
Something will remind me what we shared
what is true
what is barely left of you
Then I hear it,
a familiar whisper
and your love will come back through
Like a hope chest filled with treasures
so safely tucked away
Fingertips gently wrap them for another
lonely day

The past is really not that distant
You are there—
I only have to close my eyes
How many times will I remember?
Will your memory stay alive?
You haunt me like an old ghost story
Again
I touch your dried flowers
pressed on a fading yellow page
Delicate, beautiful and fragile
Loving words
Reread over and over
with the wind,
in the moonlight
and rain.

Acknowledgments

I am very grateful to my editor, Jessica Rothenberg, and the team at Arcadia Children's Books for making this book come to life. Thank you to J.W. Ocker for writing the foreword to this book and for his brilliant storytelling through the years. Thank you to the Amherst Historical Society, the Heritage Commission, the Cemetery Trustees, the Amherst Recreation Dept., the Amherst Dept. of Public Works, and the Amherst Town Library. I am grateful for the dedicated keepers of our precious history, such as Brian Burford, Ashley Miller, Yvette Toledo, and Dianna Wimpey from the NH State Archives; Susan Fischer, Jackie Marshall, and Katrina Holman from the Amherst Historical Society; Will and Jeanne Ludt of the Heritage Commission; MaryAnn Niles at the NH State Library; and Lisa Walker, Sarah Leonardi, Carla Ferreira, Connor Eccleston, and Amy Lapointe at the Amherst Town Library. Also, thank you to Nancy Demers, our dedicated town clerk. Thank you to local resident Steve Desmarais for his helpful memory. I am thankful for the Amherst learning community for teaching my three children. I am grateful to work with educators Sarah Strauss, Patricia Garrity, Sarah Kunyosying, Tiffany Maher, and Mary Epstein. Thank you to the Amherst residents who shared their ghost stories with me and for allowing me to share their stories.

This book is dedicated to my beloved husband, James; my three children, Vincent, Shannon, and Steven; my parents, who inspired my love for reading; and my extended family. This is especially for my sister, Shannon, and my nephews, Owen and Brandon, who love spooky tales, too. Thank you to my friend, Lisa Starnes, for helping me edit these stories. I am thankful for the kindness of my lifelong friends, Haley, Melissa, Renee, Steve & Christine, Marlene, Aldrian, Diane, Sheila, Jane-Holly, and Leni. Also, much love to my sweet book club friends: Sarah, Kim, Wendy, Lisa, and Brandie. I am grateful for all of you.

Keep believing. Happy reading.

About the Author

Susanna Hargreaves is an educator and writer in her beloved town of Amherst, New Hampshire. Susanna and her husband have raised three children and four dogs on an old, haunted road. And, yes, she believes in ghosts.

Bibliography

Bliss, GIL. "Skull found at town project may date from the 18th century." New Hampshire Union Leader* (Manchester, NH), State ed., sec. Local, 15 Aug. 2003.

Brooks, David. Telegraph. "AMHERST Renovation work at Town Hall came to a halt Wednesday when a 'turtle shell like object' found under a back corner of the building turned out to be part of a human skull." *Telegraph, The* (Nashua, NH), 15 Aug. 2003.

Britannica, The Editors of Encyclopedia. "Jeffery Amherst, 1st Baron Amherst". *Encyclopedia Britannica*, 30 Jul. 2023, www.britannica.com/biography/Jeffery Amherst 1st Baron Amherst.

Caduto, Michael J, and Joseph Bruchac. *Keepers of the Night*. Fulcrum, 1994.

Coffin, Margaret. *Death in Early America: The History and Folklore of Customs and Superstitions of Early Medicine, Funerals, Burials, and Mourning*. Nelson, 1976.

Dodge, Timothy. *Crime and Punishment in New Hampshire, 1812 1914*. American University Studies. Vol. 164. Peter Lang Publishing, 1992.

Endangered Species Act. www.fws.gov/law/endangered species act.

Farmer, Daniel Davis. *The Life and Confessions of Daniel Davis Farmer*. Printed Elijah Mansur. 1822.

Farmer, Daniel Davis. Rogers, Artemas, Reporter. Chase, Henry B., Reporter. *Trial of Daniel Davis Farmer, For the Murder of the Widow Anna Ayer, At Goffstown, On the 4th of April, A.D. 1821.* Concord [NH]: Published by Hill and Moore, 1821.

Felt, Joseph B. *The Customs of New England.* Boston: T. R. Marvin, 1853.

Hargreaves, Susanna. "Pauper's Cemetery in Amherst highlights woes in last century." *The Telegraph.* (Nashua, NH), 3, Feb. 2020.

Hargreaves, Susanna. "Skeletons in the Basement A Mystery Uncovered in Amherst." *New Hampshire Magazine*, 24, Oct. 2023.

Holman, Katrina. *Amherst Compendium of Village Old Houses. www.hsanh.org/pdfs/Amherst_Compendium_Village_OldHouses_byKH_2020Apr.pdf.

Hoornbeek, Billie. "An Investigation into the Cause or Causes of the Epidemic Which Decimated the Indian Population of New England, 1616 1619." *New Hampshire Archaeologist 19 (1976 77): 35 46.*

Johnson, Clifton. *What They Say in New England*: *A Book of Signs, Sayings, and Superstitions*. Boston. Lee and Shepard Publishers, 1897.

Kelly, Nicole. "Grisly tale of two haunted houses. The Ghost of Mack Hill Road." *Milford Cabinet*, 28, October. 1996.

Lincoln, Charles. *New England Town Affairs or The Puckerbrush Papers*. Covered Bridge Press, 1995.

Locke, Emma, P. *Colonial Amherst. The Early History, Customs and Homes*. Milford, NH., Printed by W. B. & A. B. Rotch, 1916.

Masta, Henry Lorne. *Abenaki Indian Legends, Grammar and Place Names*. Quebec: La Voix des Bois Frances, 1932.

Milford Cabinet, 24 Aug. 1893. "Amherst Jail: The Abandoned Structure Where for Years Hillsborough County Confined Her Criminals. / Built of Huge Blocks of Stone in Historic Town. / It Long Outlives its Usefulness and is to be Torn Down."

Phelps, Janet. "Ballrooms and brickwalks well become Amherst's historic houses." *Milford Cabinet,* 25, October, 1984.

Potter, C.E. *The History of Manchester.* 1856.

Redish, Laura, and Orrin Lewis. "Abenaki Legends, Myths, and Stories." *Native Languages of the Americas*, www.native languages.org/abenaki legends.htm.

Rowe, Robert and William P. Veillette. *Amherst Historical Moments.* Historical Society of Amherst, 2004.

Secomb, Daniel F. *History of the Town of Amherst, Hillsborough County, New Hampshire.* Concord, NH: Evans, Sleeper, & Woodbury, 1883.

Stimson, Pauline. *Views and Reviews of Amherst, NH.* 1988.

Walking Tours of Amherst Village. By the Historical Society of Amherst, New Hampshire. 2010.

Wheeler, Kathleen, PhD, and Chan, Alexandra, PhD. *Recovery of Human Osteological Remains at the Amherst Public Cemetery as Result of Town Hall Amherst (Hillsborough County), New Hampshire. Independent Archaeological Consulting, Inc.,* August 29, 2005.

Workers of the Federal Writer's Project of the Works Progress Administration for the State of New Hampshire. *New Hampshire, A Guide to the Granite State.* Houston Mifflin Company, Boston, 1938.